W9-AMP-301

BOOKWORMS

Color in My World

Blue Around Me

Oscar Cantillo

Cavendish
Square
New York

Published in 2015 by Cavendish Square Publishing, LLC
243 5th Avenue, Suite 136, New York, NY 10016

Copyright © 2015 by Cavendish Square Publishing, LLC

First Edition

Website: cavendishsq.com

This publication represents the opinions and views of the author based on his or her personal experience, knowledge, and research. The information in this book serves as a general guide only. The author and publisher have used their best efforts in preparing this book and disclaim liability rising directly or indirectly from the use and application of this book.

CPSIA Compliance Information: Batch #WW15CSQ

All websites were available and accurate when this book was sent to press.

Library of Congress Cataloging-in-Publication Data

Cantillo, Oscar, author.
Blue around me / Oscar Cantillo.
pages cm. — (Color in my world)
Includes index.
ISBN 978-1-50260-056-1 (hardcover) ISBN 978-1-50260-058-5 (paperback) ISBN 978-1-50260-274-9 (ebook)
1. Blue—Juvenile literature. 2. Colors—Juvenile literature. 3. Color—Juvenile literature. I. Title.

QC495.5.C366 2015
535.6—dc23

2014024959

9911

Editor: Andrew Coddington
Senior Copy Editor: Wendy A. Reynolds
Art Director: Jeffrey Talbot
Designer: Joseph Macri
Senior Production Manager: Jennifer Ryder-Talbot
Production Editor: David McNamara
Photo Researcher: J8 Media

The photographs in this book are used by permission and through the courtesy of: Cover photo by Barry Kusuma/Photodisc/Getty Images; Anna Grigorjeva/Shutterstock.com, 5; IPGGutenbergUKLtd/iStock/Thinkstock, 7; jwildman/iStock/Thinkstock, 9; ©iStockphoto.com/PhilipCacka, 11; Nengloveyou/Shutterstock.com, 13; Blend Images – Hill Street Studios/Getty Images, 15; Dallas Events Inc/Shutterstock.com, 17; MVPhoto/Shutterstock.com, 19; lixuyao/iStock/Thinkstock, 21.

Printed in the United States of America

The color blue is all around us.

It is in the sky above
our heads.

5

The ocean looks blue. Fish live in the ocean.

It is full of life.

When the ocean **freezes**, it turns into **sea ice**.

It still looks blue.

Sapphire stones are blue.

They are **treasured** for their beauty.

11

Blue jeans get their name from their color.

Many people wear them.

13

Police officers keep us safe.

They wear blue **uniforms**.

15

These blueberries are freshly picked.

They are sweet to taste.

Many animals are blue.

This blue jay has beautiful feathers.

19

Even whole mountains can look blue.

Blue is a very **majestic** color.

21

freezes (FREEZ-ez) To make liquid water into solid ice.

majestic (ma-JES-tik) Having beauty.

sea ice (SEE ISE) Giant sheets of ice on the ocean.

treasured (TRE-zhurd) Highly valued.

uniforms (YU-neh-forms) Special clothing worn by everyone in a group.

22

blue jay, 18

freezes, 8

majestic, 20
mountains, 20

ocean, 6, 8

police officer, 14

sapphire stones, 10
sea ice, 8

treasured, 10

uniforms, 14

About the Author

Oscar Cantillo is a writer. He lives near the ocean with his partner and two daughters. They all love watching beautiful shades of blue and green in the water.

About BOOKWORMS

Bookworms help independent readers gain reading confidence through high-frequency words, simple sentences, and strong picture/text support. Each book explores a concept that helps children relate what they read to the world they live in.